After Runnymede

Magna Carta in
the Middle Ages

Magna Carta Essay
General Editor : A. E. Dick Howard

Published for
The Magna Carta
Commission
of Virginia

After Runnymede

Magna Carta in the Middle Ages

Doris M. Stenton

The University Press of Virginia
Charlottesville

PREFACE

To write something new to honour the 750th anniversary of a momentous occasion seems almost impossible, for in this case our predecessors have written so much that little seems left to say. The danger is that, in the effort to find something which has not been said many times before, truth may give way to the slick new aphorism. The unfortunate phrase "the myth of Magna Carta"[1] was perpetuated, although not invented, by the discussions of the last round of celebration fifty years ago, and has bedevilled historians ever since. Stubbs, that wise old Victorian, was much nearer the mark in the phrases he has bequeathed to successive generations. Magna Carta was truly, as he said, "a revelation of the possibility of freedom to the medieval world," and there is a great deal of truth even in his statement that "the whole of the Constitutional History of England is a commentary on this charter."[2]

My indebtedness to Professor Faith Thompson's two excellent volumes, *The First Century of Magna Carta* and *Magna Carta: Its Role in the Making of the English Constitution, 1300-1629,* will be apparent to all my readers; that the former volume is now out of print is unfortunate. Professor Plucknett, whose early death

---

[1] Edward Jenks, "The Myth of Magna Carta," *Independent Review,* November 1904, p. 260.

[2] William Stubbs, *The Early Plantagenets* (8th ed.; London, 1896), p. 150, and *Select Charters,* ed. H. W. C. Davis (9th ed.; Oxford, 1913), p. 291.

we are at this moment mourning, has in his customary fashion dropped many an acute remark here and there on this, as on so many another, aspect of legal history. Concentration by modern English scholars on the Charter of King John has tended to obscure the fact that it was the Charter of 9 Henry III, with faint memories of its progenitor of 1215, which was the guiding light of the Middle Ages. To find full Latin texts in one volume of all the Charters—1215, 1216, 1217, and 1225—Blackstone is still the source to which I turn.[3]

It seems to me so important to show how laboriously the government from 1215 onwards tried to make sure that all Englishmen knew the terms of their Charter that I have tried to show how well the work of spreading information was done in the years of charter drafting, 1215-25.

DORIS M. STENTON

Reading, England
May 1965

[3] William Blackstone, *The Great Charter and Charter of the Forest with Other Authentic Instruments* (Oxford, 1759).

After Runnymede

Magna Carta in
the Middle Ages

In retrospect, the granting of the Charter of Liberties by King John in 1215 seems, after the Norman Conquest itself, the outstanding landmark in English medieval history. After this long list of liberties had been conferred upon Englishmen, nothing could ever be quite the same again. Even had John been the victor in the war of the Charter, the document, once written down and sealed, would never have been forgotten. A favourable moment would have come again in less than a generation, and in the end victory would have gone to those who opposed the King. In the century and a half between the Conquest and the struggle between King John and his barons, the new monarchy in England was consolidating its power, exercising all the rights, privileges, and authority which had belonged to the West Saxon kings, reshaping them with Norman vigour in the feudal image. It might also be said that the new monarchy, bringing to a conquered country feudal conceptions of the relations between the king and his subjects, was giving the king's authority a force and reality which no continental king had the power to maintain, or even to conceive, save in a happy dream. In 1066 England was a small and conquered country, which could be ruled by its conqueror as it could never have been ruled by its rightful king. The Anglo-Norman baronage was more tightly held in hand by the Conqueror and his sons than were any of their peers in European lands. When each of the Conqueror's sons in turn succeeded to the Crown, an attempt was made to reverse this tendency towards autocracy; each failed. The English element in the population was firmly on the King's side. Henry I's charter indicated a line of future development, but a generation of authoritative rule in a land at peace seems to have wiped out of baronial thought the pursuit of general concessions from the Crown.

Despite William I's determination to preserve the best of both laws, English and Norman, the amalgamation of Englishmen and Normans had not gone far when the first Norman generation passed. What was more important than mere amalgamation, the sparks from this fusion which might light new ideas in politics, law, and government were as yet no more than faintly struck. Perhaps they were struck too soon in Henry I's reign. His encouragement of Englishmen and his repression of his Norman barons, his heavy taxation and his new financial department with all that went with it (in particular, supervision by itinerant justices going out from and returning to the King's exchequer), meant a selfish baronial reaction when the King died leaving no son to follow him. The civil war of Stephen's reign produced no progressive ideas among the baronage, merely an impatient throwing off of the restraint of the previous reign. But the general welcome given to Henry II on

Stephen's death seems proof that the lessons of the Conqueror had not been wasted, nor even those of his sons. New ideas came thenceforward in abundance. The next struggle between the king and his subjects was fought in a very different atmosphere from that in which the Charters of Henry I and Stephen had been issued.

The half-century which preceded the grant of Magna Carta saw much that can fairly be called legislation, whether conveyed by word of mouth by the king to his ministers, granted by charter, sent by writ to the sheriffs for them to make known in their shires, or drawn up in an assize and carried through the land by itinerant justices. This last method was adopted by Henry II for the dissemination of the Assize of Clarendon in 1166, the first general eyre of the King's reign. It was increasingly employed by him as his reforming programme went ahead. But much of Henry II's legislation is irrecoverable. Apart from Domesday Book and the annual Pipe rolls, he and his ministers showed little interest in preserving a copy of the actual record of even a momentous new decision. It was for beneficiaries, whether individuals or communities, to keep their charters safe for their own sakes. Sufficient copies of the assizes through which Henry II's reforms were published must have been made for each group of itinerant justices to carry with them at least one copy when they visited each of the shires to which they were commissioned. But who shall say what happened to those pieces of parchment when the judges had finished their work? There is no one authoritative text of any of the decisions which in Henry II's reign altered dramatically and forever the administration of English law. There are signs that after 1169, when Roger of Howden began to work at his chronicle, more interest was felt in the actual letter of official

directions. At first the interest seems to be that of the
individual chronicler. Many of Howden's texts come
from Durham, and he did not succeed in filling up all the
gaps caused by his absence on Richard I's Crusade. By
the turn of the century the enrolment of charters and
other documents issuing from the Chancery was beginning, and a new attitude toward the preservation of
records was on the way. But even then it cannot be said
with certainty that the preservation of the Articles of the
General Eyres of 1194 and 1198 in Howden's chronicle
was an official act of record. It may still have been
merely the good historian obtaining copies and entering
them in his chronicle. Uncertainties like this do not
hang about the Great Charter. By long tradition it
stands as the first of English statutes.

But even in the case of the Charter, the means by
which it reached its place in the Statute Book and its
precise wording there do not make a simple story. The
most brash and optimistic rebel baron can hardly have
thought it likely that the King would fully observe all the
clauses of the 1215 Charter a moment longer than he
was forced to. The "form of security," in particular,
reckoned as chapter 61, by which the barons sought to
bind the King, inevitably exacerbated relations between
John and the rebel leaders. The baronial committee of
twenty-five to whom the future observance of the
Charter was committeed seemed to the King and his
supporters "twenty-five over-kings." In the event of the
King's breaking the terms of the Charter, they were
empowered "with the commonalty of the whole
country" to "distrain and distress Us to the utmost of
their power, to wit, by capture of Our castles, lands, and
possessions and by all other possible means, until com-
pensation be made according to their decision, saving

Our person and that of Our Queen and children."[1] The King had been forced to give to all his subjects permission to swear that they would thus aid the twenty-five to distrain and distress the King; moreover, he had been made to promise that those of his subjects who of their own free will refused to swear to aid the twenty-five in this manner he would force to do so. Distraint, the seizure of goods or chattels to enforce the payment of rent or performance of service, was the contemporary lawful means by which a lord could compel his tenants to keep their agreements with him. But turned against the King it was plain rebellion. When the Pope absolved John from his oath to observe the Charter, war inevitably followed.

The King's death in 1216 gave the barons a chance to think again under the leadership of John's own wisest counsellors. The barons had soon found that a foreign prince whom they had invited to be their king in place of John had brought with him his own followers, who regarded them as rebels to their own Lord. A drift back to their old allegiance soon began. Henry, John's eldest son, was crowned ten days after his father's death, and within a month of his coronation his advisers issued in his name a modified form of the Great Charter of English Liberties.

The Charter of 1215 is the first considerable piece of legislation initiated by subjects and discussed in detail between the king, his ministers, and a large gathering of his people. This distinction is not taken from the Charter by the fact that it was forced upon the King under threat of armed rebellion. Most of the matters

[1] For the text of Magna Carta, see A. E. Dick Howard, *Magna Carta: Text and Commentary* (Charlottesville, Va., 1964).

with which it deals had been common talk up and down the land for generations among men who had far more understanding of current legal problems than has the ordinary man of today. The local courts of justice, the shire courts, the hundred and wapentake courts, and the city and borough courts, as well as the feudal courts of the great honours and the innumerable manor courts in every shire, forced those who attended them to learn the routine of legal business. Recurrent visits of the king himself attended by a small company of judges and visits every few years of itinerant justices who sat in every shire brought the highest legal talent in the land within the sight and hearing of the common man. Most shires had within their borders royal forests which necessitated another series of courts, extremely unpopular, attendance at which was deeply resented by those who lived outside the forest but near enough to be influenced by it. No one was so humble that he could escape the routine of court attendance. Even the serf must answer for his crimes, and humble free men must be there to speak of their neighbours' repute. More substantial free men and knights must be prepared for jury work and other unpaid service. The modern scholar brooding over the chapters of the Charter, free of the romantic enthusiasm for the British Constitution felt by Stubbs, free also of the dislike of feudal barons felt by many of Stubbs's critics, free also of the conviction that of all medieval kings John was the most evil, in revolting contrast to his Crusader brother and his brilliant father, cannot but be impressed by the competence of draftsmanship in chapter after chapter, by the serious efforts which were made to survey the relations between the King, his ministers, and every class of his subjects and to provide remedies for their wrongs. That many of the chapters were careful statements of the common law which the earliest rolls of the courts of justice show in action in John's reign in no way detracts from the value of the work.

The Charter of 1215 was part of the generally recognised law of the land for but a short time. By a letter dated August 24, 1215, at Anagni, the Pope solemnly annulled it. But by the time this news reached England near the end of September the terms of the Charter had been matter of common knowledge in the remotest parts of the land long enough for men to have learned what it held for each one of them. As R. L. Poole wrote in 1913, "The charter was not merely circulated; it was proclaimed."[2] On the day the Charter itself was sealed, "19 June in the seventeenth year of our reign," royal orders were addressed, not only to all the sheriffs, but to all the King's foresters, warreners, keepers of river banks, and bailiffs, commanding that the Charter "should be publicly read and firmly held, that obedience should be sworn to the twenty-five," and that in every shire twelve knights should be chosen to make the sworn enquiries into all evil customs as the Charter enjoined. It is impossible to believe that this long document was read aloud in the shire courts in Latin. People would have rioted. They were too keenly interested not to insist on hearing and understanding the meaning of each

---

[2] "The Publication of Great Charters by the English Kings," 28 *English Historical Review* 444, 449 (1913). Poole doubts that so long a document can have been read in Latin but suggests that the same procedure as that adopted in 1258 may have been followed, that is, the reading of a statement by the King recording his agreement with the Provisions of the baronial council. I cannot help feeling that this would not have satisfied the eager listeners of 1215 and that the sheriffs must have been forced to give more detailed information in their proclamations.

provision enunciated in their own mother tongue. Much of the awe and romance which through the ages has come to surround the Great Charter was already in the ears and eyes of those who first heard its terms proclaimed and saw in the hands of the King's officer the actual document sealed with the King's great seal.

It is worth pausing for a little to consider what chapters would rouse the enthusiasm of the free men below the rank of barons and tenants in chief of the Crown who met on Lincoln Hill to hear the Charter proclaimed. The same ceremony was going on in every shire court throughout the country, but Lincoln is a good place to look back at, for the actual Charter which was read there still lies in safekeeping a few hundred yards away, in Lincoln Cathedral, and is the same document which was lent to the United States and was kept there safely throughout the Second World War. Moreover, even today it is not difficult, standing in the open space outside the castle on top of Lincoln Hill, to look back over those 750 years to the proclamation of the Charter.

Lincolnshire men were of mixed Anglo-Scandinavian blood, and Domesday Book reveals a high proportion of free men among the population of the county. In the twelfth and thirteenth centuries they were making grants of land as free men and sealing their charters with their own seals. Large numbers of the gentlemen of Lincolnshire were opposed to the King, and many of them had been among the rebels at Stamford and Runnymede. That their interest was primarily in the provisions which at last set out the legal position of the feudal tenant in relation to the King was to be expected. The barons had been defenceless against his demands for unreasonably large reliefs on entering their inheritances. Their widows had been forced to remarry at the King's bidding or, if they wished to live unmarried or choose their own husbands, pay sums so large that they were put heavily in debt. Their heirs were similarly at the King's mercy. He might give them a guardian who would waste their inheritance or reward a low-born servant with marriage to a noble heir or heiress. The Charter early deals with such matters as these, but what the King promises to his men he declares that they in turn promise to their men, many of whom were at Lincoln to hear this read out.

Although the ordinary free man would not be greatly concerned about the precise manner in which the King summoned his great Council for the assessment of a scutage or an extraordinary aid (chapter 14), there were by this date many men of modest status who owed small sums of scutage on small acreages of land. Hence the chapter which prohibited the imposition of scutage save by the common council of the kingdom and limited the imposition of aids was of widespread interest (chapter 15). Similarly, the chapters which promised protection to crown debtors, their families, and those who had stood security for the debts (chapter 9) and provisions which promised protection to those who owed money to the Jews (chapters 10, 11) were all felt to be long overdue.

In setting a reasonable limit to the amount which might be exacted from those who were subject to the King's mercy in his courts of justice all classes were considered. There was a general feeling that it should not be the court or the judges who should assess the amount that a man should pay by way of amercement, but that the amount should be assessed by men of the same sort as the payer, men, that is, who knew his circumstances and the amount he could fairly be expected to produce. This feeling resulted for earls and barons in the promise that they should be amerced by their peers and in accordance with the measure of the offence (chapter 21). Other folk, too, must be amerced in accordance with the measure of the offence; for a serious offence a man's amercement must not endanger his liveli-hood; a merchant's merchandise must not be put at risk or the serf's tillage; and no amercement must be imposed save by the oath of honest men of the neighbourhood (chapter 20).

Some of the earliest records of the king's courts of justice relate to Lincolnshire and show with what readi-ness the inhabitants of that county went to law. Their love of legal subtleties may have been in part the result of their Scandinavian blood. They would at once recog-nise the importance of chapter 38, which promised that no bailiff should henceforward on his bare word alone and without faithful witnesses put a man on trial. This was a real protection to the common man against an arrogant manorial officer, for bailiff in this chapter is certainly not confined to the king's bailiffs.[3]

When the judges visited Lincoln in 1202, in the course of their judicial circuit which took them by way of Leicester, Coventry, Northampton, Bedford, Dun-staple, and back to Westminster, many suits had been left unfinished at Lincoln and were adjourned to places farther on their journey or even to Westminster. This tiresome travelling in pursuit of the king's judges was as tedious in some trivial suit for a few acres of land as it was burdensome for litigants following up an important and fiercely contested plea before the King himself. In the Charter a real effort was made to lighten what had

[3] T. F. T. Plucknett, *The Medieval Bailiff* (London, 1954), pp. 11-13.

become a heavy burden. Common pleas were no longer to "follow our Court" but were to be held in some certain (that is, some definite) place (chapter 17), while assizes, suits which should end quickly on the verdict of a jury, were not to be heard outside the county where the land lay (chapter 18). So popular were these innovations of Henry II that the Charter laid it down that in future two justices should visit each shire twice a year to take these assizes together with four knights of the shire chosen for the purpose (chapter 18). Moreover, if on the day the shire court met to hear these actions they could not all be dealt with on the one day, enough knights and free men must stay behind to finish the work (chapter 19).

All these provisions were making new and popular arrangements, particularly popular perhaps in shires far from Westminster. Popular also must have been the promise that in future no money should be given or taken for a writ touching life or limb (chapter 36), that is, for a sworn enquiry by neighbours sought by a man accused of crime. The exact effect these new provisions would have on the working of the courts could not be immediately apparent, but what was clear to all was that in 1215 the King had been forced to look at the working of his courts purely from the litigants' point of view. What the common man on Lincoln Hill thought about chapter 34, the writ called praecipe shall not in the future be issued to anyone respecting any tenement whereby a free man may lose his court, is not easy to judge. In the past this single chapter has been taken as evidence that those who drafted the Charter wished to go back on the legal reforms of the last two generations, an argument which is clearly contradicted by the evidence of other chapters just quoted. There were many writs which began *Praecipe,* and they were increasing in number and variety. Owners of courts might well have regarded the chapter rather as a *caveat* registered on their behalf than as a ruling which would bring to an end important developments in litigation.[4]

The judicial chapters in the Charter cannot be fully discussed here, and it is certain that the men assembled on Lincoln Hill in 1215 could not immediately have taken in the full import of every one of them. But in talk after the meeting, one point after another would have been brought out, and gradually the full possibilities of the Charter would have been realised. The promises that would ensure honest and learned judges—chapter 45's "We will appoint as justiciaries, constables, sheriffs, or bailiffs only such men as know the law of the land and will keep it well" and chapter 24's "No sheriff, constable, coroners, or other of Our bailiffs shall hold pleas of Our Crown"—set out rules which the

---

[4] It certainly did not end the development of the writs of entry which began with praecipe; they multiplied in Henry III's reign. It caused the immediate introduction of a new writ of right with the phrase "because the lord has released his court to the lord king." T. F. T. Plucknett, *Concise History of the Common Law* (5th ed.; London, 1956), pp. 49-51; Doris M. Stenton, *English Justice between the Norman Conquest and the Great Charter* (Philadelphia, 1964), pp. 78-79. Miss Hurnard's conclusion in *Studies in Medieval History presented to Frederick Maurice Powicke* (Oxford, 1948), p. 179, that chapter 34 was introduced into the Charter to save tenants in chief the trouble of claiming their courts by providing an exception which the tenant could himself use has recently been challenged by M. T. Clanchy, "Magna Carta, Clause Thirty-four," 79 *English Historical Review* 542-48 (1964). There is danger in assuming from the later history of the chapter in the courts that the drafters of the Charter foresaw and intended this development.

King had tried to follow in the past and would not always be able to follow in the future, but at least the rules were there. The orotundity of such general promises as "No free man shall be taken, imprisoned, disseised, outlawed, banished, or in any way destroyed, nor will We proceed against or prosecute him, except by the lawful judgment of his peers and by the law of the land" (chapter 39) or "To no one will We sell, to none will We deny or delay, right or justice" (chapter 40) was probably taken at its face value; for these provisions were certainly inspired by immediately remembered and fiercely resented acts of violence on the part of the Crown committed during the troubled years after 1208. To each man who heard these provisions proclaimed, they probably held a different meaning. But for all men they held profound significance, a significance they never lost.

That it was only in shire courts that the Charter was proclaimed is by no means certain. The deliberate inclusion of "foresters, warreners, keepers of river banks and bailiffs" in the address of the royal writs which ordered the proclamation suggests that at least forest officials may have found themselves involved in this arduous task. The chapters promising redress of forest grievances might well be regarded as their personal concern (chapters 44, 47, 48). The grievances of cities and towns from London downwards figure early in the Charter. The aids of the city of London were to follow the rules for the assessment of baronial aids, for London citizens ranked as barons (chapter 12); but in addition all cities and boroughs were to be sure of their liberties and free customs (chapter 13). To London, of necessity, a charter was directed. There was one for the

Cinque Ports,[5] whose inhabitants also claimed to rank as barons, but other townsfolk must have depended for their knowledge of the Charter's terms on the proclamation made by the shire officials and for their protection looked to their own charters if they were so fortunate as to have them.   In view of later history it is worth remembering that, in those hectic weeks after the sealing of the Charter, knowledge of its terms was driven home to the people by proclamation throughout the land.   In the months of war, while a foreign prince was trying to gain the English throne, the Charter and its terms must have been constantly in the minds of the ordinary people of England.   It would be surprising if constant talk, now of one provision and now of another, had not convinced them that if only peace could be restored under their own king a happier future lay ahead.

The first confirmation of his father's Charter of Liberties by the young King, Henry III, is dated at Bristol on November 12, 1216.   His guardians, faithful servants of his father—Peter des Roches, Bishop of Winchester; William Marshal, Earl of Pembroke; Rannulf, Earl of Chester; Hubert de Burgh, the Chief Justiciar; and William Briewerre, outstanding among them—with the full support of the Pope given through the person of his legate, Gualo, had at once applied their minds to the terms in which the Charter should be reissued.   The speed with which the work was done in a moment of extreme national danger testifies to the Council's realisation of the importance of the Charter in the minds of all the King's subjects.   In place of the austere clauses with which John's Charter closed, the young King's advisers

[5] Though at Dover castle in the seventeenth century, it was given by Sir Edward Dering to Sir Robert Cotton and suffered greatly in the Cottonian fire of 1731.

inserted a respiting clause stating that "since some clauses in the former charter seemed weighty and doubtful, namely those concerning scutages and the assessing of aids, those concerning the debts to Jews and others, those concerning the liberty of going out and returning to our kingdom and those concerning forests and foresters, warrens and warreners, concerning the customs of counties and concerning rivers and their keepers," they are put in respite until they can be discussed at a full Council. No mention was made of the arrangements, so offensive to the King, by which the barons had tried to secure the royal observance of the Charter in the previous year (chapter 61). The omitted provisions were in the main those which might have hampered the men responsible for recovering his kingdom for the young King.[6]

Far more significant than any omissions were the verbal changes made in a number of the chapters throughout the Charter. They make it clear that from the first the King's advisers were treating the Charter as enacted law. It should be remembered that they were the supreme court of justice and individually had considerable judicial experience. They were prepared to spend time considering the best way of expressing a contentious matter so that litigation could be avoided. Wardship and dower were fertile causes of litigation. Whereas the Charter of King John promised that an heir who has been in wardship shall have his inheritance when he comes of age without relief and without fine, in

---

[6] The promise of freedom of election which John had already granted by charter to the *ecclesia Anglicana* before the issue of the Great Charter, in which he reiterated this promise, was omitted in 1216, presumably with the good will of the papal legate.

1216 it is clearly stated that the lord shall not have the wardship of the heir nor of his land before he has received his homage. After he has received his homage, the heir shall be in the wardship of his lord. Moreover, the Charter now defines the time when the heir shall come of age, "namely twenty one years," and declares that if he shall be made a knight before he comes of age he shall nevertheless remain in his lord's wardship until he is of age. The Council made a slight change of wording in the chapter (5) in favour of the guardian, who in 1216 was required to hand over the heir's estate with carts and all things at least such as when he received it whereas in 1215 the chapter had promised that the estate should be handed over "according as the season may require and the issues of the land can reasonably bear." The King in 1216 is also made to promise that "all these things shall be observed in wardships of vacant archbishoprics, abbeys, priories, churches and dignities which pertain to us; except that these wardships ought not to be sold." The 1216 Charter still promised that heirs should be married without disparagement but no longer allowed the kin a voice in the marriage, for the 1215 promise that they should be informed before the marriage was agreed was omitted (chapter 6). There was still plenty of scope for difference of opinion when any case relating to these matters should come into court.

The only changes made in the chapters concerning widows introduced a saving statement to the declaration that the widow's dower should be assigned to her within the forty days which she could remain in her husband's house "unless it [the dower] has been assigned before" and unless the house should be a castle, in which case another suitable house should be provided for her (chapter 9). While the chapters touching debts to the

Jews were omitted, those concerning ordinary debtors remained in force and were, indeed, somewhat strengthened, for the promise that land or rent should not be seized while the debtor had sufficient chattels to cover the debt was qualified by the phrase "and the debtor is ready to make satisfaction." Similarly the security of the debtor's sureties is made to depend on the willingness of the debtor to discharge the debt if he is able to do so (chapter 9).

The barons of the Cinque Ports and all other ports as well are in 1216 added to the chapter which promises protection to the liberties of the City of London and all other cities, boroughs, and towns (chapter 10). In time of war with a French prince the Cinque Ports were of prime importance to the government. Dover itself was at this very time under siege by Louis of France and defended by the Justiciar, Hubert de Burgh. The only change made in the chapters dealing with judicial eyres was that the "honest" men who were to assess amercements were to be "honest and lawful" men (chapter 15). It is possible that the council omitted chapter 45, promising that no justice, constable, sheriff, or bailiff shall be appointed except such as know the law of the land and will observe it well, because of the difficulty of enforcing it in the conditions of 1216.

The war against Louis of France necessitated several other changes of wording in individual chapters. The royal right of purveyance had in 1215 been modified to the extent that instant payment was promised unless the seller was willing to give credit. In 1216 this promise is limited to places where there is no castle. Where there is a castle, payment shall be made in three weeks (chapter 21). The seizure of horses and carts for cartage was prohibited in 1215 unless the owner agreed. In

1216, when cartage was essential for the prosecution of the war, the Charter promised that carts should not be taken without payment at the established rate, that is, ten pence a day for a cart with two horses and fourteen pence a day for a cart with three horses (chapter 23). Even with the war in progress, the Council was prepared to allow merchants free ingress and egress, but prudently added "unless they have been publicly prohibited" (chapter 34).

The speed with which the careful editing of this charter was carried out was remarkable. King John died on October 19; his son was crowned on the other side of England on October 28; the Charter is dated on November 12, in the same year 1216. It is obvious that the King's guardians must have done what they thought best to make the confirmation of the liberties granted by King John known to all the King's subjects as quickly as possible, but there is no writ ordering its proclamation surviving in the Close Rolls dated earlier than June 23 in the next year, 1217. This should cause no surprise in the troubled circumstances of Henry III's earlier months. A writ dated at Chertsey on June 23 and directed to the sheriff of Worcester runs,

We command you that on the day and place of your shire court do you cause to be read the charter of liberties which by the common council of our kingdom we have granted to our barons and all others of our realm and which the lord legate has confirmed by his seal, and the liberties contained in the charter do you cause to be observed to our faithful people within your bailliwick.[7]

[7] *Rotuli litterarum clausarum in turri Londiensi asservati,* ed. T. Duffus Hardy (Record Commission, 1833-34), I, 336. Blackstone, *The Great Charter and Charter of the Forest with Other Authentic Instruments* (Oxford, 1759), p. xxxiii, was the first historian to quote this writ, but as R. L. Poole notes (*op.*

Again, as in the previous year, the Charter of Liberties is to be read in the shire court, and again it is hard to believe that it can have satisfied the King's subjects to have it read in Latin. It can safely be assumed that in 1216 they were anxious to know how the liberties confirmed by their new young King compared with those extorted by force from his father. The men who attended the shire courts were quite capable of taking note of omissions and differences. They must have regarded the new Charter as a stopgap and awaited with interest to learn the decision of Council on such debateable matters as the forest law and the forest boundaries.

They did not have to wait long. As soon as Louis of France and his remaining baronial allies were completely defeated and peace was assured, the Council turned its attention to the Charter again. A Charter of Forest Liberties, dated November 6, 1217, took the place of the forest clauses in King John's Charter. It dealt comprehensively with grievances which had long aggravated all, of whatever rank in life, who dwelt near or needed to traverse a royal forest as well as those who possessed woods of their own which they had not been able to hunt freely or cultivate as they wished. Henceforward the Forest Charter is coupled in speech and thought with the new Charter of Liberties previously granted, although no date is put to it. The name "Magna Carta" gradually comes to be the name applied to the Charter of 1217

---

cit. *supra* note 2, p. 450n.) he erroneously gives m. 10*d* instead of m. 15*d* as the reference and reads *cartas* instead of *cartam*. Poole himself says that the construction of the writ is faulty, as it reads *cartam libertatum* and continues first with *quas* and later with *quam,* but the writ is in fact carefully and accurately drafted; the *quas* refers to *libertatum* and the *quam* to the Charter.

to distinguish it from the Forest Charter, with which it was associated in the minds of the king's subjects throughout the Middle Ages.[8] Together they formed the "Charters of Liberties," which successive kings were asked again and again to confirm.

As it had done in 1216, the Council went over the Charter, examining the wording of each chapter, sometimes adding a word or a phrase, and giving particular attention to matters which were known to give rise to much litigation. The chapter touching widows again needed modification and addition. Her husband's house in which she can remain for forty days after his death is in 1217 described as his "capital messuage," and in 1217 the Charter is more specific about the provision which must be made for her at once on her husband's death if she is obliged before the forty days are up to leave his house because it is a castle. Meanwhile, she must receive reasonable provision from the common stock. The amount of her dower is at last defined as the third part of all her husband's lands which he held during life unless she has been endowed with less at the church door (chapter 7).

Already common sense has persuaded the Council that it was beyond reason to expect justices to visit each shire four times a year to take the popular assizes. The obligation is now reduced to once a year when, together with knights of the shire, justices, no longer the specific number of two, shall take the assizes within the shire. Matters which cannot be settled in the shire court can be postponed to a place later in the circuit for settlement, and those matters which the justices cannot themselves settle shall be referred to the justices of the Bench. It

[8] A. B. White, "The Name Magna Carta," 30 *English Historical Review* 472-75 (1915); 32 *ibid.* 554-55 (1917).

seems probable that in 1215, when King John's Charter
was drawn up, those who drafted these chapters had not
realised how strongly the suitors of the shire court
resented spending more than one day upon its business.
The arrangements of 1217 were very much a reversion
to the practices of the beginning of the century.[9] But in
1217 it is provided that assizes of darrein presentment
shall always be taken before justices of the Bench, a new
ruling necessary because of the difficulties often met in
taking this assize. This is further evidence of the care
with which the revision of the Charter was made
(chapter 15). It is unlikely that, in adding the phrase
"of others than ourselves" as a definition of the villeins
whose tillage is protected from too heavy amercement,
the Council wished to make it possible for the Crown to
ruin its own tenants (chapter 12). Royal villeins were
the aristocracy of semifree tenantry. The phrase
stresses rather the saving of the humblest of the King's
subjects from starvation despite the fact that their lords
might regard them as chattels. The chapter touching
clerical amercements is tightened up and clarified by
using the phrase "no ecclesiastical *persona*" instead of
the inclusive word "clerk," by omitting the reference to
the chapters immediately preceding it, and by straightly
ordering that the parson's amercement shall not be according to his ecclesiastical benefice but according to his
lay tenement and the measure of his offence (chapter
18).

Purveyance for royal castles was still an urgent matter
in 1217, so that forty days instead of three weeks is now
allowed to constables of royal castles to pay for provi-

[9] See Introduction to *The Earliest Lincolnshire Assize Rolls*
(Lincoln Record Society, vol. XXII; Lincoln, 1926), pp. xxxv-
xxxvii.

sions (chapter 30), and it is made clear that time served
in the royal army over and above what the knight owes
for his knight's fee shall not be allowed to count towards
his exemption from castle-guard (chapter 24). The
reason for this ruling must be that knights preferred to
serve longer in the army for pay than linger unprofitably
on castle-guard. It may be assumed that where a change
of this nature is made in a chapter, a way round the
provision has been found. In previous drafts of the
Charter the King had promised that neither he nor his
bailiffs would take a man's wood without his consent. In
1217 the political situation had eased sufficiently to allow
the insertion of a provision prohibiting the seizure of the
demesne carts of ecclesiastical *personae,* knights, and
ladies by the aforesaid bailiffs, that is, those of the King
or others (chapter 26).

The chapter promising that nothing shall henceforward be given for a writ of enquiry touching life or limb
has passed hitherto from the Articles of the Barons
(chapter 26) to King John's Charter (chapter 36) and
the Charter of 1216 (chapter 29), but in 1217 a fresh
phrase makes its appearance: nothing shall be given
henceforth for a writ of enquiry "from him who seeks an
inquest touching life or limb" (chapter 32). Since the
Lateran Council of 1215, when clergy were prohibited
from taking part in ordeals, inquests touching life or
limb have taken a new significance, and the Council may
well be looking ahead at the possible implication of the
prohibition. The important reform asked for in the
Articles of the Barons (chapter 28), introduced into
King John's Charter (chapter 38), and repeated in 1216
(chapter 31) which forbade a bailiff to charge anyone on
his own mere word without witnesses is worded even
more strongly than before; in 1217 the bailiff is forbid-

den to put any man "to his open law or to an oath" without faithful witnesses produced for the purpose (chapter 34).[10] Similar clarification strengthens the wording of the famous chapter 39 of King John's Charter guaranteeing proceedings according to the law of the land. In 1216 it passed unchanged, but in 1217 the wording runs "disseised of his free tenement or liberties or free customs," a phrase which adds considerably to the force of a mere promise of protection from undefined disseisin (chapter 35).

The young King's guardians in 1217 may well have been apprehensive lest he develop as strong a determination to raise money by all possible means as his father and grandfather had shown. Fear that he might exercise the royal prerogative in regard to the wardship of undertenants of escheated honours caused them to elaborate the chapter promising that undertenants should bear no greater burdens than they would have borne had the honour been in the hands of its lord. The King in 1217 promised that he would not demand the wardship of undertenants unless they held elsewhere of him in chief (chapter 38). Similar careful foresight also probably caused the Council to define more closely the position of those who claimed the custody of a religious house. Instead of simply asserting the right of all baronial founders of abbeys who hold royal charters or who hold an advowson by ancient tenure to enjoy the wardship of them when they are vacant, the Council inserted the words "or possession" after ancient tenure (chapter 40). The question of scutage the Council

[10] W. S. McKecknie, *Magna Carta: A Commentary on the Great Charter of King John* (2d ed.; Glasgow, 1914), pp. 374-75, suggested that here again the end of the ordeal may help to account for the change in wording.

passed over in 1216 as one of the matters too difficult to
deal with at the moment.   In 1217 a clause promised
that it should be taken as it had been in the time of Henry
II (chapter 44), that is, before the great increase in the
exaction necessitated by war with France and by rising
costs.

Some important new provisions were added in 1217
which again illustrate, as do the minor changes, the
desire of the Council to make the Charter a solemn
statement of the enacted law of the land on controversial
matters.   No free man shall from henceforward give
away or sell to anyone so much of his land that he cannot
adequately perform the service due to the lord of that
fee (chapter 40), a chapter which is aimed at restraining
the fond father from overlavish provision for younger
sons and daughters.   Another new chapter dealt with an
ancient practice which had flourished even in Saxon days:
"It shall from henceforth be unlawful for anyone to
give land to a religious house and receive it back again to
hold of the house.   If anyone shall do this and be
convicted thereof the gift shall be void and the land shall
revert to the lord of the fee" (chapter 43).   A third
new chapter dealt with the longstanding problem of the
sheriff and his courts.   The shire court shall be held
monthly only, or less often if that is the custom.   The
sheriff's tourn shall be held but twice a year, at Easter
and at Michaelmas, and at the accustomed place.   The
view of frankpledge shall be held at the Michaelmas
term so that each shall have the liberties he had in Henry
II's day or has since acquired.   The view shall be held so
that the King's peace shall be kept and the tithings be
full.   The sheriff must not seek out reasons for imposing
amercements but must be content with what the sheriff
received for his view in Henry II's time (chapter 42).

Henry II, Richard I, Henry III, John (clockwise, from upper left), drawn by Matthew Paris. (Courtesy of the British Museum)

Writ of Henry III (at Chertsy, June 23, 1217) to the sheriff of Worcester directing him to read Magna Carta. (Courtesy of the Public Record Office)

Lincoln Cathedral, repository of one of the original copies of Magna Carta. (Courtesy of the British Travel Association)

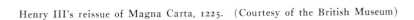
Henry III's reissue of Magna Carta, 1225. (Courtesy of the British Museum)

These are real, if perhaps fumbling, attempts at grap-
pling with hard matters which might raise questions in
the courts of law.   Chapters 40 and 43 were not the result of resentment against royal activity either in the past
or expected in the future.   They were the result of inevitable economic pressure on feudal magnates who saw
the value of their estates diminished by gifts made by
their men.   Under tenants naturally regarded the land
they held of their lords as theirs to dispose of as they
chose.   So long as land was the basis of wealth, this
problem would remain.   Even in the nineteenth century
younger sons of landed families were expected to marry
money or not at all.   These chapters look forward to the
long list of complaints presented to the King at Oxford
in 1258 by his critical baronage.

The respiting clause of 1216 was dropped, for many
of the difficult matters left untouched in Henry III's first
Charter had either been dealt with seriously or in passing in 1217.   The forest chapters had now been elabo-
rated into a weighty charter of their own.   But the
Council, in leaving as part of the royal undertaking the
promise that what the King has granted to his men they
in turn will observe towards theirs (chapter 45), added
also a chapter reserving to all archbishops, bishops,
abbots, priors, templars, hospitallers, earls, barons, and
all others, ecclesiastical as well as secular, the free customs they formerly had (chapter 46), thus leaving the
door open for differences of opinion between lord and
man.   Finally, in this charter the end of the war is cele-
brated by an order that all adulterine castles built or rebuilt during the barons' war shall be destroyed.   Again,
as in 1215 and 1216, directions went out to all the sheriffs to make the Charter known through meetings of
their shire courts.   General directions were not des-

patched until February 12, 1218, although the Charter
was certainly sealed in the autumn of the previous year.
The Great Charter is undated, but the Forest Charter
was sealed on November 6, 1217. "We send you,"
wrote the King to the sheriff of Yorkshire,

the charters of liberties granted to all of our kingdom
as well touching the forest as other matters, commanding that you cause them to be read publicly in your
shire court having called together the barons, knights
and all free tenants of the same shire, who shall there
swear fealty to us. And do you diligently, paying attention to each point in the charters, cause them to be
sworn and observed in all things, and particularly that
clause which is put at the end of the Great Charter
touching the destruction of adulterine castles, built or
rebuilt since the beginning of the war.[11]

Again, as in 1215 and 1216, to read the King's Charters to the people in Latin would have been useless,
neither would it have fulfilled the King's commands.
The contents of what can henceforward be called
"Magna Carta" were driven home by this constant
reiteration by the King's representatives in their shire
courts. The 1218 writ seems even to command an
explanation of each point in the Charters to the people.
When in 1225 Henry III was at last able to see his own
new great seal affixed to a third royal confirmation of his
father's grant of liberties, he stated at the beginning of
the Charter that he issued the Charter of his own free
and spontaneous will, and at the close he recorded that
for "the grant and gift of these liberties and of others
contained in our Charter of liberties of our forest the
archbishops, bishops, abbots, priors, earls, barons,
knights, free tenants and all others of our kingdom have
given us the fifteenth parts of all their moveables." The
chapter ordering the destruction of adulterine castles

[11] Hardy, ed., *op. cit. supra* note 10, I, 377.

was omitted, but nothing new was promised. The time of drafting new chapters was over.[12] The King's advisers had tried to turn the Charter into a code of law which could be amplified, modified, and kept up to date, but they had learned that it could not be done. The law was moving too quickly for them.

There had been a pause in legal development while the Charter war was in progress. Even before that, when the interdict shocked the country in 1208 and when in 1209 King John lost the services of many of his clerical judges who could not bring themselves to serve an excommunicated king, legal development had begun to falter. King John did his best to keep his courts of justice working, but even the support and help of his lay judges could not suffice to maintain the Bench at Westminster and judicial eyres throughout the land.[13] The growth of the common law depended on the continuous activity of the royal courts of justice. With the re-establishment of the Bench at Westminster and the sending out of the great general eyre of 1218-19, which was completed in 1221-22, the banked-up fires broke out and legal development surged forward. But it was a natural and, indeed, inevitable development, more effective than any attempt to remodel the Charter into a code of law. The traditional numbering of the Charter is henceforward into thirty-seven chapters.

The establishment of what in the event became the

[12] It should be noticed that by the time Magna Carta came to be enrolled on the Statute Roll in 1297 the amount of a baron's relief—which was "at the King's will" in Glanville's time, £100 in the Charter of King John and in those of Henry III, and 100 m. in Bracton's view (f. 84)—had been reduced to the last figure, which is that of the text of Edward I's *inspeximus* of the Charter. See C. Bémont, *Chartes des libertés anglaises* (Paris, 1892), p. 47n.4.

[13] See Stenton, *op. cit. supra* note 4, pp. 88-114.

final text of the Charter marked a change in the general
attitude to it. That it had been extorted by war from a
reluctant king was not forgotten, nor was it forgotten
that King John had been the original grantor. But the
purchase of the 1225 Charter from a willing royal seller
by a generous financial aid set the pattern for the future.
The Charters of Liberties (common liberties and forest
liberties) had become the fundamental part of the law of
the land, that part valued above all other aspects of the
law, that part which was written down in documents to
which appeal could be made. In any crisis, when a hard-
pressed king needed supplies for war, when reform of
abuses was demanded by the people but delayed by the
Crown or by individual ministers, a cry could be raised
for the confirmation of the Charters.

But despite the constant reiteration of the Charters'
chapters, there always was a certain confusion about
precise details. This is evident from the way the St.
Albans chroniclers, Roger of Wendover and Matthew
Paris, wrote. They had lived through the years of
charter drafting and knew intimately the great men
concerned in public affairs. Yet they seemed to think
that the Charter of 1225 was in no way dissimilar to that
of King John. Those who heard the Charter proclaimed probably fastened on the chapters which particularly concerned them and left the full picture to be filled
in by others. The common memory of the English
nation may well have held all that the Charter had ever
granted them from 1215 to 1225. Matthew Paris, in
describing in 1255 how it "was proclaimed in shire courts
and announced in synods, in churches, and everywhere
where men met together that the Great Charter should
be inviolably held," describes it as the *magna carta*
"which King John granted and the present king has

many times confirmed." He was uninterested in the
differences between John's Charter and those of his son.

There can be no doubt that it was the constant reiteration of the terms of the Charter, during the years that it
was taking its final shape, which secured its place in the
minds of the men of all classes, churchmen and laymen,
great magnates and knights of the shire, citizens and
burgesses, the ordinary free man and the unnumbered
villagers, the semifree and the serf, who made up the
population of England, as their security against arbi-
trary government, whether they feared it from the King
or his ministers, from their lord or his bailiffs. Magna
Carta was there to be appealed to. It was for the King's
subjects to appeal to it by demanding that it should be
again confirmed. The future history of the Great
Charter was already implicit in the issue of 1217. Its
later history begins with the Charter of 1225.

But already the first general eyre after the war had
gone out through England, and at least one monastic
chronicler associated it with the Charter of King John.
It began in November 1218, and under the year 1219 the
Waverley annalist records that "after Christmas justices
commonly called itinerant went through all England
watching over the restoration of the laws and causing
them to be observed in their pleas according to the
aforesaid charter of King John."[14] That the judges
took care to see that no unduly heavy amercements were
imposed in accordance with the Charter is evident from
the surviving records of proceedings, but they did not
find it necessary to refer to the Charter itself as their
authority for pardoning poor men who had fallen into

[14] *Annales Monastici,* ed. H. R. Luard (Rolls Series, 1864-
69), II, 291.

the King's mercy.[15]   The judges who visited Yorkshire
came near to it since they frequently pardoned amercements imposed on the poor "for the king's sake."[16]
Whether the judges in Yorkshire accepted on the King's
behalf any of the offerings of half a mark made by men
accused of homicide or assault to have the verdict of a
jury is difficult to determine, for the list of amercements
has not survived.   Since there are no notes that sureties
were taken for the payments, it seems probable that with
chapter 26 in mind they allowed the accused to have a
jury without payment.[17]

   Occasionally a chapter in King John's Charter which
had been omitted from later issues was long afterwards
appealed to in a plea, rightly and with success.   A tenant
in a Herefordshire case arising from disseisin pleaded in
19 Edward I that the tenements in question were in the
Marches of Wales and therefore should be dealt with by
Marcher law and not by English law "according to the
Statute of Ronemede."[18]   The charter sealed at Runnymede may also find an occasional reflection in a private
grant which does not refer by name to King John's
Charter: the phrase "rendering thence a penny in scu-

[15] It had been customary to do this in the early years of John's
reign; see *The Earliest Northamptonshire Assize Rolls, 1202-
1203*, ed. Doris M. Stenton (Northamptonshire Record Society;
London, 1930), V, cases 859, 917, 931.
[16] *Rolls of the Justices in Eyre for Yorkshire, 1218-19* (Selden
Society, vol. LVI; London, 1937), see "Index Rerum" under
"amercements."
[17] *Ibid.*, cases 557, 570, 724. This chapter is 36 of the 1215
Charter; 29 of Henry III's first Charter; 32 of his second
Charter; and 26 of his third and final version.
[18] Quoted by C. H. McIlwain, in "Magna Carta and the Common Law," *Magna Carta Commemoration Essays*, ed. H. E.
Malden (London, 1917), p. 136, from *Abbreviatio Placitorum*,
p. 1051.

tage, namely when scutage is given in the kingdom by the common council of the realm" can only refer to chapter 14 of the Charter of 1215.[19] When in 1231 an enquiry was held into the liberties of the royal manor of Heddington and the hundred of Bullingdon, it was said that formerly the sheriff had come only once a year to make view of frankpledge and attachments touching pleas of the Crown but after the making of the Charter of Runnymede the sheriff came twice a year to do these things; here there is evident confusion between the Charters of 1215 and 1217.[20] The sheriff's view was mentioned for the first time in chapter 42 of the 1217 Charter.

The common law received in Magna Carta its first generally recognised statute, written law, authoritative at the date of its publication. But the common law could not stand still. New problems were continually arising which needed new remedies or the modification of old ones. While there was a general determination to hold the Charter as unalterably authoritative, it was faced with an equally strong tide bringing change, which could sometimes be dealt with in the courts as the cases came up without the enunciation of published statements, but often—more frequently as years went by—needed discussion in the King's Council, resulting in the compilation and publication of written statutes. Some of these must make changes in the law as defined in the Charter even if they do not directly contradict it.

The extraordinary thing is that, whether by chance or as a result of the skill of the original drafters of the Charter, its clauses seem to have been so worded that

[19] *Duchy of Lancaster Misc. Books* I, 258 (MS in Public Record Office, London).
[20] *Curia Regis Rolls* (London, 1961), XIV, no. 1185.

only definite repeal would destroy their validity. It was often definition and addition, not repeal, that was needed. Did not Parliament itself, in confirming Magna Carta in 1368, declare that all acts contrary to it were void? By this time enactments had in effect rendered void many of the Charter's provisions, but after 1368 lawyers did not as a result of the confirmation of that year ignore the statutes which had repealed parts of the Charter.[21] The spirit of the Charter, its general intention, if not all its detail, was irrepealable. By 1236 it was already necessary to issue statements in Council touching matters which had also concerned the drafters of Magna Carta. For instance, the Statute of Merton gave the widow right to damages if deprived of her dower; it gave her also power to bequeath the standing crops upon her dower land. The publication of this statute, made famous by the baronial refusal to change the law of England and so legitimise children born after the marriage of their parents, marks the continuation of the process, begun by the Charter, of issuing a written statute after discussion between the King and his barons. By 1236 changes in the law could no longer take the form of a charter, or even an assize. Before long the form was to be that of statutory legislation by Parliament, and other folk than the King's immediate council and his tenants in chief were to be involved.

The difficulty of interpreting individual chapters in the Charter was being brought home to the King's advisers in the years immediately preceding the Great Council at which the Statute of Merton was discussed and set out. The famous chapter 39 of the 1215 Charter (chapter 35 in 1217 and 29 in 1225), promising

[21] T. F. T. Plucknett, *Statutes and Their Interpretation in the Fourteenth Century* (Cambridge, 1922), p. 27.

proceedings according to the law of the land together with the seemingly straightforward promise to the lords of felons' lands that the King will retain them only for his customary year and a day, after which the lands shall be returned to the lord of the fee, had proved in need of elaboration. A carefully worded directive in the Close Rolls for August 1234, addressed, significantly enough, to the sheriff of the litigious county of Lincoln, informs him that in future no one taken for homicide or any other felony shall be disseised of his lands, tenements, or chattels before conviction, but by view of the coroners, the sheriff or his bailiffs, and the bailiffs of the accused his chattels shall be enrolled and his bailiffs shall give security to answer for their value, reserving to the accused and his family while he shall be in prison their reasonable maintenance. If the accused should prove guilty of felony, his chattels, apart from what had been necessary to provide for him and his family while he was in prison, should remain to the King together with his land for the customary year and day. If he is proved not guilty, his chattels shall remain to him quit. The marginal note to this entry is *touching liberties.*[22]

Another of the chapters in the Charter gave the Council considerable trouble in the same year and had probably been under discussion in more than one meeting, and for more than one year, before the writs of this year were despatched. They look back to a Lincolnshire case heard at the Bench and marked by Bracton for his *Note-Book.*[23] Maitland made it famous by his commentary.[24] The sheriff of Lincoln appeared at the Bench in 1226

[22] *Close Rolls 1231-34* (London, 190<), pp. 587-88.
[23] *Note-Book,* III, case 1730; now printed in *Curia Regis Rolls* (London, 1957), XII, cases 2142, 2312.
[24] Frederick Pollock and F. W. Maitland, *History of English Law before the Time of Edward I* (2d ed.; Cambridge, 1923), I, 549-50.

with four knights of the shire charged to report on the difficulties the sheriff had met in trying to settle the large volume of litigation awaiting hearing in the shire court. Under the leadership of two troublesome knights, who demanded that the sheriff observe the promises made by the King in his Charter, the suitors refused either to spend more than one day on the business of the court or, when the sheriff postponed the suits to the occasion of his view through the ten wapentakes of Ancaster, to deal with the pleas there, basing their refusal on the Charter.

In the Bench no decision was reached, but a considerable space was left on the roll, the two recalcitrant knights withdrawing "without day by the king's command to await his summons."[25] The matter seems to have rested there, but at the end of August 1234 writs were sent out generally to the sheriffs pointing out that the King's Charters granting liberties and free customs had been made to all men great and small of his kingdom and the Charters remained in every shire; further, the King willed that, as his magnates desired that he should keep the terms of those Charters in regard to them, so should they keep them in regard to their men. He therefore commanded that proclamation should be made, throughout the shire, that hundred courts, whether in the hands of the King or others, should only be held twice a year, as the Charter declares.

But further directions were necessary, and on October 11 in the same year 1234 a writ was addressed to the sheriff of Lincoln "touching the interpretation of the little clause contained in the liberties, how it should be understood," as the marginal note in the Close Roll describes it. It runs as follows:

Since we have heard that you and your bailiffs and also the bailiffs of others who have hundred courts in your

[25] *Curia Regis Rolls* (London, 1957), XII, case 2312.

shire do not understand how the hundred and wapentake courts in your shire ought to be held after we
granted to all of our kingdom the liberties contained in
our Charters which we made while we were under age,
we have caused the same Charter to be read recently in
the presence of the lord of Canterbury and the greater
and wiser part of the bishops, earls and barons of our
whole kingdom so that this little clause contained in
our Charter of liberties could be expounded by them,
namely that no sheriff or bailiff should make his tourn
through the hundreds save twice a year, and only in
the accustomed place and manner, namely once after
Christmas and again after Michaelmas without trou-
bling people, so that each shall have at least his liberties which he had and used to have in the time of
King Henry our grandfather, or had acquired since;
therefore it was there said by many that in the time of
King Henry our grandfather as well hundreds as wapentakes and the courts of magnates used to be held every
fortnight.   And although it would greatly please us for
the common welfare of our whole kingdom and to provide for the welbeing of the poor, nevertheless since
those two tourns do not suffice to keep our peace and to
correct the excesses as well of the rich as the poor,
which is the work of the hundred courts, it is provided
by the common counsel of the aforesaid lord of Canterbury and all the aforesaid bishops, earls, barons and
others that between the aforesaid two tourns, hundred
and wapentake courts and the courts of magnates shall
be held every three weeks, where they used to be held
every fortnight; provided that no general summons is
made to those courts as is made to the aforesaid tourns,
but to those hundreds, wapentakes and other courts
there shall come the plaintiffs and their adversaries
and those who owe suit, through whom pleas can be
held and judgments made; unless it shall be that at
those hundreds or wapentakes an inquest touching pleas
of the crown ought to be made, such as homicide or
treasure trove or something of that sort; to such in-
quiries there shall come, with the aforesaid suitors, the
four neighbouring villages, namely all from those vil-

lages who are needed to make those inquests. And
therefore we command you that the aforesaid hundreds,
wapentakes and courts, as well ours as those of others,
shall be held from henceforth according as is aforesaid
every three weeks, except for the aforesaid two tourns,
which shall be held henceforward as they used to be
held before. Witness the king at Westminster 11 October.[26]

This elaborate statement to explain one "little clause" of
the Charter makes it easy to understand why, when the
business at Merton in 1236 was put in writing, no
attempt was made to turn any of the decisions into a
charter or to add them to the existing clauses of the
Charter of 1225.

In the meantime relations between the King and his
barons were already tense, since the King was determined to rule through ministers of his own choice and
according to his own mind. The barons were equally
determined to hold what had been won by the Charter
and to claim more voice in discussion of general policy
and in deciding the amount of financial help the King
could expect from his subjects. The Charter was constantly invoked by both sides, for the King never hesi-
tated to remind the baronage that by it they were as
closely bound in regard to their men as he was to
them.

As soon as he became fully of age in 1227, the King
began to look into the way the Forest Charter had been
interpreted during his minority, showing more skill than
might have been expected in so young a man. He made
no attempt to repudiate the Charter of the Forest, but
ordered fresh perambulations to be made of forest
boundaries, for the disafforestations made in accordance

[26] *Close Rolls 1231-34,* pp. 588-89.

with the Charter had included not only forests newly made by Henry II, but areas restored by him to the forest after illicit disafforestation in the anarchy of Stephen's reign. In accordance with the Charter, the King made no attempt to claim for the forest those areas which his grandfather had newly afforested, but he restored to it those woodlands which Henry II had himself restored. Moreover, Henry III succeeded, through the later troubles, in retaining the forest boundaries as he had established them after the perambulations of 1227. In return for a thirtieth of movables, the Forest Charter, together with the Great Charter, was confirmed again in that year, and Edmund Rich, Archbishop of Canterbury, excommunicated all who should violate the Charters. In 1253, in return for an aid from the barons and a tenth from the Church, the Charters were again confirmed, and against all who should transgress them a sentence of excommunication was pronounced.

That the Charters had stimulated discussion about the rights and duties of a king is beyond dispute. From very different sources the same impression comes that men were thinking about problems of government with a new intensity, even if they couched their argument in the language of the Psalms, Roman law, or John of Salisbury's *Policraticus*.[27] The difficulty of controlling the expanding army of officials necessary for the increasingly complicated business of ruling a much-governed land was growing. It was no longer on the sheriffs alone that criticism about oppression needed to centre. To name no others, escheaters were a constant source of complaint, for the general promises in the Charter about the

[27] Fritz Schultz, "Bracton on Kingship," 60 *English Historical Review* 136-76 (1945).

safeguarding of the lands of heirs were ill observed, as always.

During the years between 1236, when the King brought home his French wife, who was followed to England by her impecunious kinsfolk and their many able clerks, and 1258, the year of the baronial rebellion, a volume of criticism was building up about the King's dependence on the Pope, his favour to foreigners, his employment of foreign clerks, his debts, his reafforestation of the old forests, and the abuses in local government which were going uncorrected. Whether Bracton himself, who had acted as a judge of the King's own *coram Rege* court, was the author of the famous outbreak in his treatise need not be considered here, since it clearly expresses a deeply felt contemporary opinion:

The king has a superior, namely God, also the law through which he has been made king; also his court, namely earls and barons, for they are called earls (*comites*) because they are the king's companions, and who has a companion has a master. And therefore if the king is without a bridle, that is without law, they ought to put a bridle on him . . . .

The writer, whoever he was, simply expressed what many men thought who had meditated on what the Charter had won for every class. The reference to the earls and barons who should put a bridle on a tyrannous king surely meant that the Charter was in the mind of the writer.[28] *The Song of Lewes*, written after the King's defeat in 1264, stresses again and again that the King must keep the law: "If the king be without law he will go astray; if he hold it not he will err shamefully.

[28] *Ibid.*

Its presence gives right reigning, and its absence the disturbance of the realm."[29]

The Barons' War was preceded, as the Charter war had been, by the drafting of a long list of matters for which the barons sought redress. The first complaint begins with the statement, "The earls and barons seek *petunt . . . ,*" and each of the following twenty-eight plaints with the phrase, "They also seek a remedy . . . ." The list sets out very reasonable demands for the reform of matters ranging from inheritance and relief; the infiltration of foreigners, the dangers that may arise from allowing them to hold castles (particularly upon the sea coasts), and a demand that heiresses shall not be married to foreigners, "men not of the nation of the realm of England"; the forests; mortmain; the conduct of judicial eyres; the exactions of sheriffs; the relations of feudal courts with one another and with the royal court; to complaint that the King has granted so many quittances to knights, allowing them to avoid jury service, that in some counties no grand assize can be taken for default of knights.

Carefully studied, this long list of complaints not only displays the political uncertainties of the day but also reveals how much more complicated the law of the land and local government have become with the passing years. The baronial criticisms of 1258 were a natural development from those of the previous generation in 1215. But the barons have become more sophisticated. They can now ask for a remedy about marriage portions, describe them as "not absolute but conditional gifts," and complain that women who have received them and

[29] *The Song of Lewes,* ed. C. L. Kingsford (Oxford, 1890), p. 52.

have no heirs give away or sell their portions. The barons plead for the means of recovering such settlements for the family inheritance by "a writ of entry or something of that sort." This provision may well be, as Plucknett says, "inexpertly drafted" and it deals with only one of the problems raised by such gifts,[30] but it is a sign that baronial thought has fully accepted all the implications of royal justice.

The Provisions of Oxford, drawn up by a baronial committee, was perforce accepted by the King, and his acceptance was proclaimed throughout the land in October 1258. He did not order that the full text of the baronial reforming plan should be proclaimed, or even at the moment made known to his subjects. It could not be, for the full results of their deliberations were to be revealed as decisions were reached, and the baronial committees worked on steadily through 1258 and 1259. The barons were capable of examining the state of the nation as a whole and intended to do it. In the Provisions of Westminster of November 1259, they added important decisions to those of the previous year. Henry III's proclamation that whatever the elected council did should be established forever was made through letters patent sent to each shire in Latin, French, and English.[31]

This order shows that the sheriff was expected to make all in his shire—the clerkly element, those who commonly used French, and the English population of the countryside—know what the King had been forced to command. That the sheriffs in 1215 had been expected to inform all men of the gist of the Charter can be safely asumed, although no one had time to write an English

[30] T. F. T. Plucknett, *Legislation of Edward I* (Oxford, 1949), p. 131.
[31] Poole, *op. cit. supra* note 2, p. 450.

or French version for the sheriffs' use. Those who
drafted the Provisions of Oxford were at one in the
statement, "Let the Charter of liberty be firmly kept."[32]
To the chronicler Rishanger it seemed that the Provisions were themselves based on the Charter.[33] Throughout the Barons' War the Charter was frequently referred to. Even King Louis of France in his attempt to
compose the quarrel in 1264 stated that, while the Provisions of Oxford which the Pope had already declared
void should be annulled, he in no way intended "by" his
"present order to weaken in any way the royal privileges,
charters, liberties, statutes and laudable customs of the
realm of England which had existed before the time of
those provisions."[34]

When the King had been defeated by Simon de Montfort at Lewes and the King and his son were in baronial
custody, a solemn confirmation of the Charter was issued, apparently on March 8, 1265, and the Berkshire
copy was laid up at Reading Abbey, where the monks
had it copied in full into the cartulary with their title
deeds.[35] As Richard Thomson, whose excellent book on
the Charter published in 1829 is now all too little used,
remarks in discussing the settlement between the King,
his son, and Simon de Montfort after the battle:

The most remarkable part of this Confirmation, is
the clause which was evidently formed upon the 61st
chapter of the Great Charter of King John . . . ex-
cepting that it contains no provision for the safety of
the royal family. It states that if the King or his son

---

[32] William Stubbs, *Select Charters,* ed. H. W. C. Davis (9th
ed.; Oxford, 1913), p. 386.
[33] William Rishanger, *Chronicle,* ed. J. O. Halliwell (Camden
Society; London, 1840), pp. 16-17.
[34] Stubbs, *op. cit. supra* note 32, p. 397.
[35] B.M. Harl, MS 1708 f.7.

shall not keep the preceding conditions . . . it shall
be lawful for all of our kingdom to rise against us,
and to harass us and our possessions by all means in
their power; to which by our present precept we will
oblige all and everyone, notwithstanding the homage
and fealty which they have done to us; so that they observe us in nothing, but that all consider how to distress
us, as if they held of us in nothing, until proper satisfaction has been made . . . .[36]

King John's Charter was no longer confirmed, but it had
not been forgotten.

That the victory of the future Edward I over the
barons at Evesham in 1265 and the clearing up of the
rebellion by the Dictum de Kenilworth were not followed by any reversal of the reforms secured during the
period of rebellion was essentially due to the wisdom of
Edward himself.   He had shown himself receptive to
new ideas when Simon de Montfort began his propa-
ganda but had been persuaded to oppose the rebels by
the necessity of upholding the position of the Crown.
When he himself was in control, he saw to it that the
Parliament at Marlborough in 1267 put the baronial
achievements into statutory form.   This is the first of
the great Edwardian statutes, for although Henry III
did not die until 1272 he was already spent.   The Great
Charter and the Forest Charter, already confirmed in
the Dictum de Kenilworth, were again confirmed in
chapter 5 of the Statute of Marlborough:

The Great Charter shall be observed in all his Articles
as well in such as pertain to the King, as to others;
and that shall be enquired afore the Justices in Eyre in
their Circuits, when need shall be, and afore sheriffs in
their counties when need shall be, and writs shall be

[36] Richard Thomson, *An Historical Essay on the Magna Carta
of King John* (London, 1829), pp. 377-79.

freely granted against them that do offend, before the
King, or the Justices of the Bench, or before the Justices in Eyre when they come into those parts.   Like-
wise the Charter of the Forest shall be observed in all
his Articles . . . .[37]

But there was no setting out of the Charter in detail.

Nevertheless, in 1279 Archbishop Pecham in his
council at Reading ordered not only that all violators of
the Charter should be excommunicated but also that the
Charter itself, well and truly copied out, should be
posted in all cathedral and collegiate churches and the
copies renewed from time to time.   But this was going
too far, and the king ordered the removal from church
doors of copies of Magna Carta.   The Charter had by
now become incorporated into the common law.   It was
the common law's most sacred and inviolable part.

The reign of Edward I was the turning point.   He
and his learned judges, with his great men, clerk and lay,
in Parliament, were making new law which the courts
would have to enforce, interpret, and develop.   A vast
volume of new law set out in elaborate statutes, the
precise effect of which the judges themselves did not
always foresee, was massively enforcing the old common
law in every direction.   The judges themselves were not
always sure of the texts of the new statutes and tended to
rely on their memory of their wording.   They occasionally had to send for the statute before making their
judgment.[38]   The barons and commonalty were even
more uncertain.   In these circumstances, they clung to

[37] Translation in *The Statutes at Large* by Danby Pickering
(Cambridge, 1762).
[38] Plucknett, *op. cit. supra* note 21, pp. 103ff.   The great Justice Bereford said to a party, "Show us the statute," and when he
had seen it told them that they were not in the case provided for
in it.   *Ibid.,* p. 104.

the Charter as to a lifeline holding them to clear and simple expositions which they could understand and with which they and their fathers had been long familiar. Hence in 1297, when Edward's financial demands on his subjects, clerical and lay, had reached such heights that rebellion seemed possible, the King offered to confirm the Charters, but the bishops and barons demanded safeguards beyond the formal confirmation of the past.

They wanted new provisions, as simple and direct as those of the Charter, prohibiting the new taxation to which all objected, to be added to the Charter itself. In the *Confirmatio Cartarum,* granted by the King's son and the Council with him in London and by the King himself later at Ghent, he promised that the Charters should be kept in every point; that copies should be sent under seal to justices and sheriffs, to all other officers, and to all cities with royal writs ordering the publication and observance of the Charters; that judgments given contrary to the points of the Charters should be annulled; that archbishops and bishops should twice a year pronounce sentences of greater excommunication upon all who did not observe all points of the Charters; and that the Charter should be read twice a year to the people. New chapters were drafted, promising that no extra taxation should be taken without consent, but they were never actually incorporated into the sacred text.[39]

It was at this crisis that the Great Charter found its place in the Statute Book as an *inspeximus* by Edward I in the twenty-fifth year of his reign, that is, in 1297. The Forest Charter was inspected at the same time and put in the statute book with the Great Charter, for,

[39] A careful scrutiny of the chronicle evidence about the so-called statute "de tallagio non concedendo" was made by Professor H. Rothwell, "The Confirmation of the Charters in 1297," 60 *English Historical Review* 16-35, 177-91, 300-15 (1945).

despite the careful perambulations in the early part of
Henry III's reign, people were dissatisfied with the
established boundaries, as well as with the behaviour of
the forest officials. Edward I ordered commissioners to
enquire into complaints against officials in 1298, and in
1299 and 1300 commanded that perambulations of forest boundaries should be made. As a result of these
perambulations, made by people interested in disafforestation rather than the King's rights, the King was
obliged in the Lincoln Parliament to authorise the
disafforestation of areas outside the newly perambulated
boundaries. He was able to revoke these concessions
with papal support in 1305, but his son and grandson in
their days as king each in turn was forced to go back to
the boundaries accepted by Edward under pressure at
Lincoln in 1300.[40]

   After almost a century of confirmations and threats of
excommunication against violators and the formal inclusion of the Charter as a statute in the written volume of
new law which the thirteenth century and particularly
the years of Edward I had created, it might almost seem
that the process of confirming the Charters had been
reduced to a common form and could have meant little.[41]

---

[40] G. J. Turner, *Select Pleas of the Forest* (Selden Society,
vol. XIII; London, 1901), pp. ciii-cvi.

[41] For the number of times the Charter was confirmed, see
Faith Thompson, *The First Century of Magna Carta: Why It
Persisted as a Document* (Minneapolis, 1925), Appendix C,
p. 116, and *Magna Carta: Its Role in the Making of the English Constitution* (Minneapolis, 1948), pp. 9ff (hereinafter cited
as Thompson, *Magna Carta*). She makes the point that the traditional list of confirmations does not include all of them by any
means. Sir Edward Coke's "Thirty-two acts of Parliament"
are far too few. Some confirmations have merely a passing note
in a chronicle. Some probably escaped mention at all. Professor
Thompson gives the recorded list of confirmations. *Ibid.,* p.
10n.4.

On the other hand, it is clear that no class or social group, neither the Church nor the barons, neither cities nor towns, neither individual knights of the shire nor free men, could let the Charters lapse into a mere formula of heedless confirmation. The freedom of the Church, the liberties of London, the rights of individuals in a variety of situations, were nowhere else so clearly and succinctly set out, and set out in terms which a simple laymen could understand. Valuable additions had since been made to elucidate the feudal law as it concerned crown tenants and consequently the tenants of these royal tenants in chief. The Cinque Ports and other towns found it better to rely on their own royal charters than to plead that their liberties were derived from the blanket grants of the Great Charter.

Inevitably the very simplicity of statement in the Charter offered opportunities for argument in the courts of law. But it was essentially the direct, straight-forward statements of the Charter which made it so eminently quotable and memorable. Long before its use by seventeenth-century lawyers in their struggle with the Stuarts, both sides in national quarrels were quoting chapter 29 of the 1225 Charter in a way which the seventeenth-century folk would have understood: "No freeman shall be taken or imprisoned . . . . To no man will we sell or refuse or delay right or justice." Professor Faith Thompson found that in the wide range of sources she used more references were made during the fourteenth century to this famous chapter than to any other in the Charter. The individual phrases of this chapter—"nor will we go upon him nor send upon him," "the lawful judgment of his peers," "the law of the land"—by their frequent use in violent quarrels between successive kings and their magnates acquired new meanings in the legal vocabulary and prepared the way for the arguments of the seventeenth century.

Throughout the Middle Ages, despite the growing volume of new law and new writs to provide remedies for old wrongs, references were being made to chapters of the Charter. They are less frequent in the plea rolls, because all the arguments and the give and take between judges and pleaders are not recorded. But in the Year Books, those who were taking notes in court thought it worthwhile to record even lines of argument which pleaders dropped when they saw that they would not win acceptance. In the early fourteenth century private petitions were still being entered on the parliament rolls, and petitioners were happy to quote the Charter when they thought it relevant to their cases. Professor Thompson has collected several such references. Sometimes those who quote the Charter bend it to their purpose by misquotation. In 8 Edward II the men of Cornwall ask that the King's ministers and others in Cornwall use the same weights and measures as are used elsewhere in the kingdom according to the provision in the Great Charter,[42] which is not quite the same thing as chapter 25. Nor was an heir entirely justified, when asking for proper provision for himself from the issues of his estate, in saying that the Charter declares that the guardian is charged with the duty of sufficiently maintaining the child therefrom. But as Professor Thompson points out, the petitioner is at least representing the spirit and implications of the Charter.[43]

Plucknett, in noticing how frequently it appeared that even the judges were ignorant of the precise wording of a statute in the fourteenth century, remarked that, if the

[42] Thompson, *Magna Carta*, p. 40.   [43] *Ibid.*

court itself was so ill equipped with the tools of its work, pleaders "would seem to have been even less favourably placed."[44]   Presumably even pleaders practising in the courts depended for their knowledge of the Charter on memory, unless they were so fortunate as to possess one of those little manuscript collections of statutes beginning, as they usually did, with the Charter.[45]

That the judges in eyre in 1218-19 were observing the Charter's promise of reasonable amercements or, in the case of poor folk, none at all, in accordance with chapters 20 and 21 of King John's Charter, has already been noted.[46]   The popularity of this provision, chapter 14 in the 1225 Charter, continued through the years, although it was occasionally used in a somewhat surprising fashion.   Barons, according to chapter 14, should be amerced by their peers and according to the measure of the offence, but the barons of the Exchequer, who as early as 1202 undertook the task of assessing the amercements to be paid by barons,[47] tended to set them higher than barons were always willing to pay.   In 1322 the Abbot of Croyland, and in 1326 Thomas de Furnival, succeeded in obtaining writs directing that they should be amerced according to the provision of the Great Charter.[48]

William Dugdale, in giving a long account in his *Baronage* of the eminently baronial family of Furnival, notices with some surprise that although Thomas de Furnival was commanded to attend the king with horses and arms to march against the Scots and to attend all the Parliaments of Edward II and some of Edward III he was yet not a baron, as the writ of Edward II proves.

[44] Plucknett, *op. cit. supra* note 38, p. 104.
[45] Thompson, *Magna Carta*, p. 38.   [46] *Supra*, pp. 31-32.
[47] *Op. cit. supra* note 9, XXII, case 173.
[48] Thompson, *Magna Carta*, pp. 40-41.

This writ, which Dugdale quotes, is addressed to the
Treasurer and barons of the Exchequer pointing out
that, although Thomas is not a baron, he has been
amerced as one, to his loss.[49] Edward I and his advisers,
realising the popularity of the rules touching amercements, repeated and strengthened them in the first Statute of Westminster: "And that no city, borough nor
town, nor any man be amerced, without reasonable cause
. . . ,"[50] and stated that amercement should be "by his
or their peers." By the early fourteenth century the
tenants in courts leet and courts baron were in enjoyment
of this protection, and a number of writs "touching a
reasonable amercement" were available which according
to Fitzherbert were "founded upon the Statute of
Magna Carta, cap. 14."[51] "By the Statute of Magna
Carta every amercement in Court Baron ought to be
affeered by two Tenants of the Manor upon Oath."[52]

Litigants in a lord's court were also interested in
chapter 28, forbidding a bailiff to put anyone to his law
or an oath on his bare word without credible witnesses.
The use of the word "bailiff" is important here, for it
covers the lesser royal officials in the shires who were,
under the sheriff, in charge of the hundred courts as well
as the lord's officers in villages and manors, who might
thus put men to their law in the courts baron. By the
fourteenth century the chapter could be used to prevent
bailiffs allowing civil pleas to go forward when the
plaintiff had brought no adequate proof, although it

---

[49] *The Baronage of England* (London, 1675), I, 726.
[50] Thompson, *Magna Carta,* p. 44.
[51] *The New Natura Brevium* (London, 1687), p. 167.
[52] *Ibid.,* p. 170. These writs are not the only ones which Fitzherbert traces to chapters in "the Statute of Magna Carta."
See, *e.g.,* writ of *ne injuste vexes* (*ibid.,* p. 21); *writ de rationa-
bili parte bonorum* (*ibid.,* p. 270).

seems probable that its original intention was to protect men accused by the bailiff in criminal cases on his own bare word alone.[53] Plucknett regarded chapter 28 as the logical extension to lay courts of Henry II's legislation, in Normandy in 1159 and in England in the Constitutions of Clarendon in 1164, against officials in ecclesiastical courts who proceeded against laymen without any other accuser than themselves.[54] This chapter had a long history, for the introduction of the word *juramentum*, oath, in the 1217 Charter "made it possible for the Puritan lawyers in Elizabeth's reign to use the provision as a defence against the oath ex officio" in the church courts.[55]

As the Middle Ages drew to an end, the Charter sank into the background in the courts of justice. So much new law had been made that it was rarely helpful to cite a legal dictum from the remote past, although pleaders still used the Charter occasionally for making "frivolous exceptions" which carried no weight with judges. Nevertheless, the most popular of the Charter's chapters, those which had been quoted again and again through the centuries, were still well remembered and revered: notably chapter 9, the liberties of London; chapters 11 and 12, common pleas and assizes and where they may be heard; chapter 14, reasonable amercements; chapter 29, lawful judgment of peers; and chapter 35, local courts. The interpretation put on them would not necessarily be that of the contemporaries of those who had drafted them. Judges themselves were not always of one mind in their interpretation. Those learned lawyers who were writing about the law in the Tudor age were well

[53] Thompson, *Magna Carta*, pp. 56-57.
[54] Plucknett, *op. cit. supra* note 3, p. 12.
[55] Thompson, *Magna Carta*, p. 56.

aware of the important place that the Charter held in the history of legal development. Christopher St. Germain's *Doctor and Student*, Fitzherbert's many-times-reprinted and enlarged work on legal process, and above all Lambarde's *Eirenarcha*, written for the guidance of justices of the peace, and his *Archeion*, a commentary on the high courts of justice in England, all display the realisation that the Great Charter lies at the very heart of all that is most to be valued in English law. But it is not of the Charter of Runnymede that these learned lawyers thought and to which they referred, but the Charter of 9 Henry III, with which their collections of Statutes began.[56]

It is true to say that to the Elizabethans it probably seemed that the Charter had done its work as a practical force making for the liberty of the subject, his good government, and his fair treatment in the courts of law. Nevertheless the Charter remained to them a subject to arouse both interest and national pride. At the beginning of the sixteenth century Richard Pynson, in origin a Norman, set up as a printer in England and in 1508 became the King's Printer. Very early in his career in England he had produced an edition of the *Antiqua Statuta or The Boke of Magna Carta*. A translation of the Charter with other statutes appeared in 1534. Early editions were poor, and even the Charter was

[56] "In this plight that High Court of the King continued, until that *Henry 3*, in the *ninth* yeare of his Reigne . . . finding by experience that it was either chargeable or dilatory, or both, for his subjects to have no other remedy for tryal of their *rights* . . granted unto his Subjects the great Charter of the Liberties of *England,* in the 11. *Chapter* whereof he ordained thus, *communia Placita* . . . ." *Archeion; or, A Commentary upon the High Courts of Justice in England* (London, 1635), pp. 41-42. This work was completed by William Lambarde in 1591. *Dictionary of National Biography* (London, 1950), XI, 493.

not complete, but improvements soon came. Richard Tottel, printer in 1569 of the first and so far the most beautiful edition of Bracton's great book on English law, printed also a new edition of the *Antiqua Statuta,* which Sir Edward Coke used.

It has been stated and is still occasionally repeated that the fact that Shakespeare "does not say a word about" the Charter in his play on *King John* was a sign that the Charter was forgotten.[57] It is merely evidence that he did not regard it as good theatre.

[57] C. E. Petit-Dutailles, *Studies and Notes Supplementary to Stubbs' Constitutional History* (Manchester, 1905), I, 130, quoting A. F. Pollard, *Henry VIII* (London, 1905), pp. 33ff.